OUR FATHER
AND THE
HAIL MARY

Nihil Obstat: Right Reverend Archimandrite Francis Vivona, S.T.M., J.C.L.
Imprimatur: Most Reverend Joseph A. Pepe, D.D., J.C.D.
Date: March 18, 2014

By Bart Tesoriero
Illustrated by Miguel D. Lopez

catholic
children's
CLASSICS

ISBN 978-1-61796-137-3

Artwork and Text © 2014 Aquinas Kids, Phoenix, Arizona
Printed in China

Our Father

Our Father, who art in heaven,
hallowed be Thy name.
Thy kingdom come,
Thy will be done, on earth as it is in
heaven.
Give us this day our daily bread;
and forgive us our trespasses,
as we forgive those who trespass
against us;
and lead us not into temptation,
but deliver us from evil.
Amen.

Our Father, Who Art in Heaven, Hallowed Be Thy Name

In the beginning, a long, long, time ago, before the world was made, even before there was the sky, or the sun, or the moon, there was God! God alone!

God wanted to share His goodness, so He started creating things. He made the sun, the moon, and the stars, and He liked what He saw. So He kept going! He made the earth, with its trees and plants, birds, fishes, and all the animals. God looked at His creation, and He said, "It is good!"

Then God created Adam and Eve, the first humans. He said, "Now that is very good!" Sadly, Adam and Eve disobeyed God, and they lost His presence in their hearts. But they did not lose His love.

God sent His Son, Jesus, to become one of us. He gave his life for us on the Cross, so that we could once again know God's love for us and feel His love in our hearts. Jesus taught us that God is our Father—our "Daddy!" God loves us very much and wants us to get to know Him.

Jesus taught us a special prayer to pray to God. We call it the "Our Father." When we pray, "Hallowed be Thy Name," we are saying, "God, we love You. You are wonderful! May Your Name be praised always."

5

Thy Kingdom Come, Thy Will Be Done On Earth as it Is in Heaven.

Heaven is where God dwells. It is a happy place because God shares everything. It is His Kingdom, and Jesus is the King!

Jesus came to bring God's Kingdom to earth. He did this by healing people who were sick. He brought the Kingdom by teaching people about His Father in heaven. Jesus gave people the power to love one another as He loved them.

When you feel good, and when you feel happy, where do you feel it? Many of the people who saw Jesus felt the peace and joy of God in their hearts. They felt His healing power.

This is the Kingdom—the place in us where Jesus is King! Jesus taught that the Kingdom of God is very small, like a tiny seed, when it begins in us. If we water this seed with our love and prayer and good deeds, then it will grow inside our hearts and become like a great tree.

When we pray "Thy Kingdom come," we are asking God to live in our hearts so that we will want to do what He wants for us. We are asking God to help us care for the poor and those who have less than we do. We are asking God to help us forgive our brothers and sisters.

Give Us this Day Our Daily Bread

God is our Father. He wants to feed us and care for us, because we are His children. Jesus teaches us to ask God each day for what we need. When we speak to God, He listens to us. God hears us every time we pray.

When Jesus was on earth, people traveled a long way to see Him. One time many people had been with Him all day, and they were hungry. The only one with any food was a little boy who had some bread and fish. He gave his food to Jesus. Jesus took the loaves and the fish, looked up to heaven, and blessed them. Then He gave the food to the people. The people kept eating, and the bread and fish kept multiplying! Everyone ate their fill, and there was even food left over. Just as Jesus had promised, God provided what was needed.

God knows that we need food for our bodies. He also knows we need food for our hearts and our souls. Jesus gave us Himself as our living bread. We receive this Bread of Life when we receive the Body of Christ in Holy Communion. In Holy Communion, Jesus comes into our hearts.

And Forgive Us Our Trespasses, As We Forgive Those Who Trespass Against Us

Sometimes we make mistakes. Sometimes we disobey God. Sometimes we hurt other people by what we do. Guess what? Everyone does these things. That's why we all need to forgive each other every day!

Just as we ask God for our daily bread, we also need to ask Him to forgive us when we disobey Him. We need God to forgive us when we sin against Him or others.

God loves to forgive us, and to hold us close to Himself. A very special way to receive God's forgiveness is in the Sacrament of Reconciliation, where Jesus forgives us through the priest. He takes away all our sins and then forgets them! However, Jesus wants to do more for us. He wants to heal us. He wants to touch our hearts where they hurt, and to put His love right there! The more of God's love we have in our hearts, the better we feel.

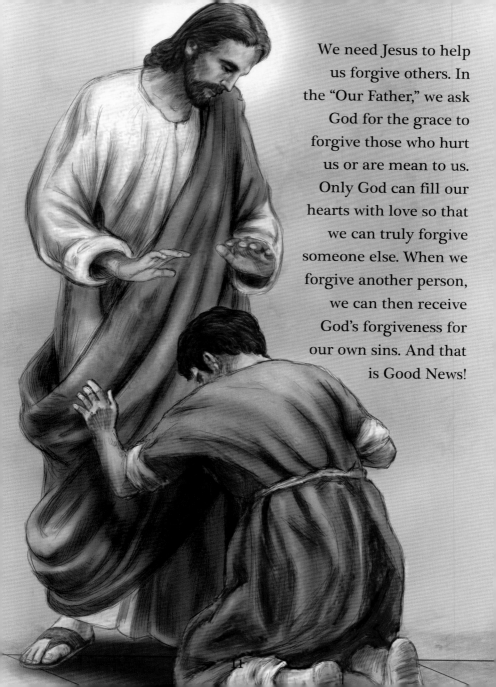

We need Jesus to help us forgive others. In the "Our Father," we ask God for the grace to forgive those who hurt us or are mean to us. Only God can fill our hearts with love so that we can truly forgive someone else. When we forgive another person, we can then receive God's forgiveness for our own sins. And that is Good News!

And Lead Us not into Temptation, But Deliver Us from Evil. Amen.

Jesus is the Good Shepherd. A good shepherd knows his sheep by name. He watches over them, and leads them to grassy meadows and pools of water. His sheep know him, and they follow him, because they recognize his voice.

In this part of the "Our Father" we ask God to be with us in a special way. We ask Him to lead us on a safe path. We ask Him to keep us from the way that leads to sin. We also ask God to give us His love in our hearts. If we love God with all our heart, then we will do our best to follow Him. God promises us that He will never allow us to be tempted too much. He will always help us and show us a way out. Let us continue to ask God to help us avoid sin. Let us ask God to help us especially at the hour of our death.

As we end this prayer, we ask God to deliver us from evil and the evil one, who is the devil. The devil cannot hurt us, as long as we stay close to Jesus and Mary and the saints and angels. We belong to God now, and God keeps us safe.

We close our prayer
with "Amen," which
means, "I agree!"
We do agree with
Jesus as we pray
this prayer to
Our Father.

13

The Hail Mary

Hail Mary, full of grace,

the Lord is with thee.

Blessed art thou among women,

and blessed is the fruit

of thy womb, Jesus.

Holy Mary, Mother of God,

pray for us sinners,

now and at the hour of our death.

Amen.

Hail Mary

A long, long time ago, there lived in Israel an elderly couple named Joachim and Anne. After many years, God heard their prayers for a child. Anne gave birth to a lovely little girl, whom they named Mary.

Mary was a beautiful little girl. She loved to help others. She fed the birds and cared for the little creatures that played in her yard. As she grew older, Mary helped her mother to cook and bake. Mary played happily with her little friends. Everyone in Nazareth loved her bright eyes and her cheerful smile. She brought joy to others wherever she went. In time, Mary grew into a young lady.

Joseph was a carpenter in Nazareth. One day he met the lovely young Mary. She was modest, yet very kind. Joseph and Mary grew to love each other, and decided to marry. They became engaged, and were called man and wife even though they did not yet live together.

Soon afterwards, God sent the angel
Gabriel to Mary. He appeared to Mary,
and greeted her. "Hail, Mary, full of grace!
The Lord is with you." Mary was surprised
to see the angel. She thought to herself,
"What sort of greeting is this?" We also
greet Mary by praying, "Hail, Mary!"

Full of Grace

The angel Gabriel said to Mary, "Do not be afraid! You have found favor with God. Behold, you will conceive a son in your womb, and you shall call him Jesus. He will be great, and he will be called the Son of the Most High God. He will rule over the people of Israel, as did his ancestor, King David, long, long ago!

When Mary heard these words, she felt happy and excited, yet also a little afraid. She said to the angel, "How can this be? I am a virgin! I am not yet married." The angel replied, "The Holy Spirit will come upon you, and the power of God will overshadow you. The child to be born of you will be holy, the Son of God. Look, Elizabeth your cousin, has also conceived a son in her old age. Nothing will be impossible with God." Mary said, "I am the handmaid of the Lord. Let it be done unto me according to your word." Then the angel left her.

When we pray the "Hail Mary," we repeat to Mary the words of the angel. "Hail Mary, full of grace. You always obeyed God. You always wanted to please Him. He loved you and filled you with His grace from the very first moment you were alive in your mother's womb!" This pleases Our Lady very much. She loves God and she loves us.

The Lord is with Thee.

The angel Gabriel told Mary, "The Lord is with you." Why did he say that?

Do you remember Adam and Eve? They had lost the presence of God in their hearts. But God did something very special for Mary. He put His presence into her heart before she was born! The Lord was with Mary from the very first moment of her life inside her mother's womb. God made Mary pure from the very beginning of her life. He did that because someday He would ask her to become the mother of His Son, Jesus. God wanted His pure and holy Son to be born from a woman who was pure and holy from birth.

Many years before, a holy man named Isaiah had told the Jewish people that the Lord would give them a sign. He said that a virgin would give birth to a son. His name would be "Emmanuel," which means "God is with us." When God is with us, we feel full of joy and peace. We feel safe, because God is with us, and He is stronger than anyone else in the world!

God sent Jesus to take away all of our sins. Now He puts His presence into our heart through our Baptism. He makes us pure like our Mother in heaven.

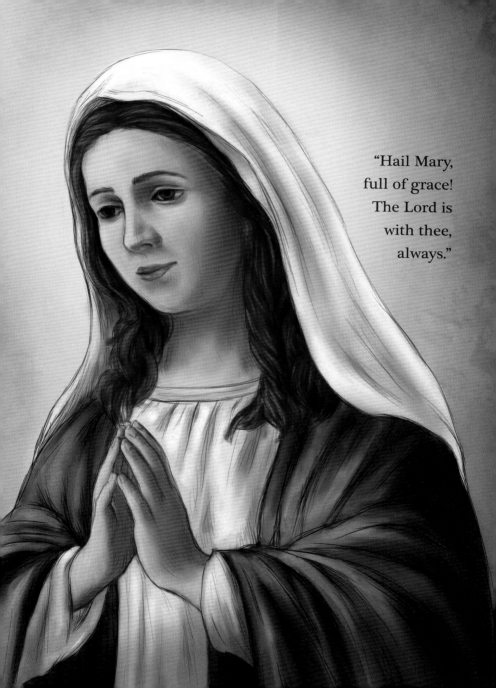

"Hail Mary, full of grace! The Lord is with thee, always."

Blessed Art Thou among Women

After the angel left her, Mary went to visit her cousin Elizabeth and her husband Zechariah, who were both very old. Mary wanted to help them prepare for the birth of their baby, who would be Saint John the Baptist. God had chosen him to prepare the way for Jesus.

After traveling for some days, Mary arrived at their home, and greeted Elizabeth. When Elizabeth heard Mary's greeting, the baby inside her womb jumped for joy! Elizabeth was filled with the Holy Spirit. She cried out in a loud voice, "Blessed are you among women, and blessed is the fruit of your womb! Who am I that the mother of my Lord should come to me? For the moment your greeting reached my ears, the baby in my womb leaped for joy. Blessed are you who believed that what the Lord promised you would come true!"

Mary felt her own heart leap for joy when she heard Elizabeth. She cried out, "My soul magnifies the Lord, and my spirit rejoices in God my savior! Behold, from now on all ages will call me blessed."

We do call Mary blessed every time we pray the "Hail Mary." Mary shares her blessings with all of us whenever we ask her help. She is our dear Blessed Mother!

And Blessed Is the Fruit of Thy Womb, Jesus.

Joseph and Mary lived in the country of Palestine. The Romans ruled Palestine at the time. The Roman ruler, Caesar Augustus, had ordered all the people of Israel to return to their home towns for a census. Joseph and Mary traveled to the city of David, called Bethlehem, because Joseph was of the house and family of David.

They arrived in Bethlehem late one night. Mary was very tired, but they found no place to stay. Finally, Joseph found a little stable with a manger in it where the animals were fed. On that holy night, Mary gave birth to her son, Jesus. Mary wrapped Baby Jesus in warm clothing and laid Him in the manger, where it was warm.

The angel of the Lord appeared to shepherds who were watching their sheep in the nearby fields. The angel said, "Do not be afraid! Behold, I bring you good news of great joy: Today in the city of David a Savior is born for you who is Messiah and Lord."

Jesus is the fruit of Mary's womb. He is blessed because He is the Son of God. We are also blessed because Jesus lives in our hearts.

When we pray, we draw near to Jesus and Mary. God wants to bless us. He wants us also to be a blessing to others, as His Son Jesus is a blessing to us.

Holy Mary, Mother of God

God made Mary in a very special way. Her soul was always pure. Mary received this grace from God and then obeyed Him always. That is why we call her holy.

Mary grew as God's friend. Like you, she had to go to school and learn about new things, so her mind could grow. Like you, her body grew as she got older, just like your body is growing. Most of all, her heart grew every day, more in love with God.

Mary is the Mother of Jesus. Jesus is both God and man. Therefore Mary is the Mother of God!

Mary worked very hard at the little home in Nazareth. She woke up early every morning to bake bread and prepare breakfast for her family. She went to the well every day for water. She tended the garden and cleaned the home. She baked the bread and prepared the meals. She was busy!

Jesus gave Mary to us. She is our Mother now, too. It is good to ask our Mother Mary to help us obey God and become holy. A holy person is someone who lets God love them. A holy person takes time to pray and be with God.

God loves you. Talk to Him often. He likes to hear from you! Ask Mother Mary to help you love as God wants you to love. Ask her to help you be like her son, Jesus.

Pray for us Sinners

God created Adam and Eve to be happy with Him. However, the devil tempted them to disobey God. Adam and Eve sinned when they turned away from God. Because of their sin, sadness and suffering came into our world.

God sent His Son Jesus to live for us, to die for us, and to rise from the dead so that we could live a new life in Him. Jesus died on the cross for us, because He loved His Father, and because He loves us.

Sometimes it is hard to obey God. All of us have done what we wanted instead of what God wanted. We have not always loved God or each other. Sometimes we have been unkind. We have not included others in our play. Sometimes we have disobeyed our parents. We may have been unkind to our sisters or brothers. In this way we have sinned.

That is why we ask our Mother Mary to pray for us. Mary understands us. She loves us so very much. She helps us each time we pray. She helps us to feel God's love in our hearts and to be joyful.

Dear Mother Mary, please pray for us!

Now, and at the Hour of Our Death. Amen.

After Jesus died, some of His friends placed His body in the arms of His Mother Mary. Mary felt very sad as she held Jesus. She remembered how she had held Him as a little baby, so close to her heart. Now He could not speak any more. He could not hear any more. Mary wept.

Our Mother Mary cares for us very much, just like our own mothers. She talks to God about us all the time. She asks God to protect us, to lead us, and to guide us. Of course God already wants to do these things for us, but He likes to be asked, as we all do.

When we pray the "Hail Mary," we are praying as God wants us to pray. We are asking our Mother to please pray for us now, to go before God for us. We also ask Mary to pray for us at the hour of our death. None of us knows when we will die. We hope it will be a long time from now! We want Mary to help us at the hour of our death, as she helped her son, Jesus. We pray now for this grace. That way, no matter what happens, God will be with us.

God loves us! We belong to Him. Let us ask Our Mother Mary to pray for us, now and at the hour of our death. Amen.